ON BLISS

JOSEPH CAMPBELL ESSENTIALS

ON BLISS

JOSEPH CAMPBELL

JOSEPH CAMPBELL™
FOUNDATION

New World Library
Novato, California

New World Library
14 Pamaron Way
Novato, California 94949

Text design by Tona Pearce Myers

Library of Congress Cataloging-in-Publication data is available.

First printing, September 2025
ISBN 978-1-955831-10-9
Printed in Canada

10   9   8   7   6   5   4   3   2   1

New World Library is committed to protecting our natural
environment. This book is made of material from well-managed
FSC®-certified forests and other controlled sources.

IF YOU FOLLOW your bliss, you put yourself on a kind of track that has been there all the while, waiting for you, and the life that you ought to be living is the one you are living. Wherever you are—if you are following your bliss, you are enjoying that refreshment, that life within you, all the time.

MYTHOLOGY OPENS the world so that it becomes transparent to something that is beyond speech, beyond words, in short, to what we call transcendence.... But what is beyond? Even the word *beyond* suggests a category of thought! So transcendence is literally transcendent. Of all knowledge. In the Kena Upanishad, written back in the seventh century B.C., it says very clearly, "that to which words and thoughts do not reach." The tongue has never soiled it with a name. That's what transcendent means. And the mythological image is always pointing toward transcendence and giving you the sense of riding on this mystery.

SOCIAL PRESSURE is the enemy! I've seen it happen. How in heaven's name are you going to find your own track if you are always doing what society tells you to do? I also spent a year teaching in a boy's prep school and that was a crowd that was trying to make up their minds, you know? I've seen them since and those who followed their zeal, their bliss, they have led decent, wonderful lives; those who did what Dad said they should do because it's safe found out it's not safe. It's disaster.

THIS IS AN ABSOLUTE necessity for anybody today. You must have a room, or a certain hour or so a day, where you don't know what was in the newspapers that morning, you don't know who your friends are, you don't know what you owe anybody, you don't know what anybody owes to you. This is a place where you can simply experience and bring forth what you are and what you might be. This is the place of creative incubation. At first you may find that nothing happens there. But if you have a sacred place and use it, something eventually will happen.

IN THE SANSKRIT, there are three terms that bring you to the very brink of the transcendent: *sat*, *cit*, and *ananda*. *Sat*—"being": In your living you can't possibly know what the experience of being is. You're having an experience, but is it being? *Cit*—"consciousness": But is my consciousness of myself, or my consciousness of consciousness actually the ultimate of consciousness? But *ananda*—"bliss"—you can know. And I say your bliss, your rapture, is your guide to transcendence. Follow your bliss, and all the archetypes will come flocking to you.

IF YOUR BLISS is just your fun and your excitement, you're on the wrong track. I mean, you need instruction. Know where your bliss is. And that involves coming down to a deep place in yourself.

I HAVE A FIRM belief in this now, not only in terms of my own experience, but in knowing the experiences of other people. When you follow your bliss, and by bliss I mean the *deep sense of being in it*, and doing what the *push* is out of your own existence—it may not be fun, but it's your bliss and there's bliss behind pain too. You follow that and doors will open where there were no doors before, where you would not have thought there were going to be doors, and where there wouldn't be a door for anybody else.... And so I think the best thing I can say is follow your bliss.

...**BUT THEN** you also have moments of ecstasy. The difference between everyday living and living in those moments of ecstasy is the difference between being outside and inside the Garden. You go past fear and desire, past the pair of opposites...into transcendence.

A GOOD LIFE is one hero journey after another. Over and over again, you are called to the realm of adventure, you are called to new horizons. Each time, there is the same problem: Do I dare? And then if you do dare, the dangers are there, and the help also, and the fulfillment or the fiasco. There's always the possibility of a fiasco. But there's also the possibility of bliss.

THAT'S ONE of the monastic disciplines, where you go to sleep pronouncing a mantra of waking knowledge—kind of a fishing line to carry you from waking to transcendent consciousness. But the fact that the Buddha means "the one who has waked up" teaches the main lesson here. The way in which the metaphor of sleep and waking is used relates to exactly that state. The Buddha has awakened to that undifferentiated consciousness. From that point of view, we who have not waked to that are asleep in our rational, normal, and even dreaming lives. That awakening is the great breakthrough.

THE RETURN and reintegration with society, which is indispensable to the continuous circulation of spiritual energy into the world, and which, from the standpoint of the community, is the justification of the long retreat, the hero himself may find the most difficult requirement of all. For if he has won through, like the Buddha, to the profound repose of complete enlightenment, there is danger that the bliss of this experience may annihilate all recollection of, interest in, or hope for the sorrows of the world; or else the problem of making known the way of illumination to people wrapped in economic problems may seem too great to solve. And on the other hand,

if the hero, instead of submitting
to all of the initiatory tests, has, like
Prometheus, simply darted to his goal
(by violence, quick device, or luck) and
plucked the boon for the world that
he intended, then the powers that he
has unbalanced may react so sharply
that he will be blasted from within and
without—crucified, like Prometheus,
on the rock of his own violated
unconscious.

INDIVIDUALISM IS perfectly fine if the individual realizes that the grandeur of his being is that of representing something. Even representing a system of ideals and images that the rest of the world, and the environment, doesn't have; he still is the agent of something and he is a presence. But when the individual is acting only for himself or for his family or for his team, then you have nothing but chaos.

ANY LIFE CAREER that you choose in following your bliss should be chosen with that sense—that nobody can frighten me off from this thing. And no matter what happens, this is the validation of my life and action.

PEOPLE SAY that what we're all seeking is a meaning for life. I don't think that's what we're really seeking. I think that what we're seeking is an experience of being alive, so that our life experiences on the purely physical plane will have resonances within our own innermost being and reality, so that we actually feel the rapture of being alive. That's what it's all finally about, and that's what these [myths] help us to find within ourselves.

WHERE IS YOUR BLISS station? You have to try to find it. Get a phonograph and put on the music that you really love, even if it's corny music that nobody else respects. Or get the book you like to read. In your sacred place you get the "thou" feeling of life that [Indigenous] people had for the whole world in which they lived.

NOW, AS I'VE gotten older, I've been thinking about these things. And I don't know what being is. And I don't know what *consciousness* is. But I do know what *bliss* is: that deep sense of being present, of doing what you absolutely must do to be yourself. If you can hang on to that, you are on the edge of the transcendent already.

I REMEMBER when I was a student in Paris, at the University of Paris. I was studying philology—how Latin and vulgate Latin become transformed into French and Spanish and Italian. I was sitting in the little garden at the Musée de Cluny on Boulevard Saint Germain, and I thought to myself, "What use is all this knowledge to me, when I don't even know how to order a decent meal?" So I looked for the place where my bliss was, where I felt my life was, and that academic thing dropped off.

MY WORD for young people now who ask me is, follow your bliss. It will come. Nobody's ever been on that road before, and so, where you didn't know there were doors, there are not only doors but palaces.

WHENEVER A KNIGHT of the Grail tried to follow a path made by someone else, he went altogether astray. Where there is a way or path, it is someone else's footsteps. Each of us has to find his own way. Nobody can give you a mythology. The images that mean something to you, you'll find in your dreams, in your visions, in your actions—and you'll find out what they are after you've passed them. No one in the world was ever you before, with your particular gifts and abilities and possibilities.

THE ENIGMATIC SAYING of Jesus that "the Kingdom of Heaven is within you" intended this same sort of idea. When you have that view, you rest, so to say, in yourself—in your deepest part, within the bounds, to use theological terms, of God. And He speaks to you from within yourself. If you throw the God image away, as one does in Buddhism and ultimately in Hinduism, you will immediately recognize that whatever the power is that we speak of as divine operates from within as the source, and you can have faith in your own nature.

TO BE REALLY HAPPY in life one has to relax into a grand spell of utter laziness every so often—and this spell should be punctuated with not too violent spurts of enthusiasm.

THERE IS this wonderful theme of the Five Sheaths in the *anandamaya* culture in India, that life is an expression of bliss. The Five Sheaths are sheaths that enclose the mystery of the life germs. . . . The ultimate sheath within is the Sheath of Bliss. *Anandamayakosha.* All life is driven by bliss.

WITH THE CRUCIFIXION, if you think of this as a calamity that is the result of your sins and Adam's sin and all that, that Jesus had to come down, the Son of the Father, give himself up on the Cross for death, and look sad there—that's one reading. But you can read it another way: as the zeal of eternity for incarnation in time, which involves the breaking up of the one into the many and the acceptance of the sufferings of the will as part of the organic delights, the Wisdom Sheath and rapture, the bliss—he is in bliss. St. Augustine says this somewhere,

where he says, "Jesus went to the Cross as the bridegroom to the bride." That's a total transformation of the idea.

HOW DID [JUNG] do it? He went back to think about what it was that most engaged him in fascinated play when he was a little boy. So that the hours would pass and pass. Now if you can find *that* point you can find an initial point for your own reconstruction. Go back and find what was the real fascination. So Jung went back to boyhood and found that he loved to play with stones, making little villages. Then he went and bought

himself a piece of property and began, with his own hands, building that amusing little castle that he had there in Bollingen on Lake Zurich. Now each one has to work it out in his own way. But if a person just refuses to think that he has an inside problem, he's not going to work the thing out. Nobody can do it for him. You have to learn how to recognize your own depths.

MICKEY HART and Bob Weir [of the Grateful Dead] ... invited Jean and me to an event in Oakland that just became a dance revelation. I got something there that made me note that this is magic. And it's magic for the future. ... They hit a level of humanity that makes everybody at one with each other. It doesn't matter about this race thing, this age thing, I mean, everything else dropped out. ... It was just the experience of the identity of everybody with everybody else. I was carried away in a rapture. And so I am a Deadhead now.

THE RELIGIOUS PEOPLE tell us we really won't experience bliss until we die and go to heaven. But I believe in having as much as you can of this experience while you are still alive.

A WOMAN in West Virginia, in the coal-mining areas there, ... in her late sixties had the dreadful feeling that she had lost life, that she had never lived life, that there had been a life for her that she had not lived. And in the analysis they found one time when she was a little girl, about thirteen years old (that's about the time for the experience), she was walking in the forest and she heard a strange music, a strange song. But she didn't have in her culture the assistance to help her do something with that and so she lost it. And then throughout her life she had the feeling that she hadn't lived her life. The thing about the shaman crisis is that if the individual does not follow the song he will die, he will really die.

BRAHMAN IS the Sanskrit way of talking about [the transcendent]. Manitou is the Algonquin, Orenda is the Iroquois, Wakan Tanka is the Sioux.

THE WAY TO FIND out about your happiness is to keep your mind on those moments when you feel most happy, when you really are happy—not excited, not just thrilled, but deeply happy. This requires a little bit of self-analysis. What is it that makes you happy? Stay with it, no matter what people tell you. This is what I call "following your bliss."

THE MIND up here thinks it's in pain and in trouble and the body's saying, "No, sir, you're in bliss, only you just don't know it." The function then of mythology is to connect you to your bliss and find where it truly is. When you get yourself off course or you accept some moral principle that is altogether cockeyed and related to something that isn't natural at all, dismiss it and follow the bliss.

THE SIMPLE TASKS of our life, when you're doing them because they're a function or factor in the life that you love and have chosen and have given yourself, then they don't weigh you down.

THE FOURTH FUNCTION of mythology—and this is the one where you suddenly feel the lack of myth today—is the *pedagogical*, the guiding of individuals in a harmonious way through the inevitable crises of a lifetime. That's the main one. Linking the individual to his society so he feels an organic part of it. The individual is carried by the myth in a very deep participatory way into the society and then the society disengages him. And so what happens to all his energy? It has to go down deep into himself, and that is the mystical part, the interrelation to the life cause. First induction of the individual into

the society; then disengagement
of him and the carriage of him
through mystical meditations and the
understanding of the symbols to the
seat of his own life within himself.

IN MYTHOLOGY the deity becomes transparent to transcendence—and you also, at the same time—and then comes that wonderful fun, that wonderful exhilaration of identification with the very energy that is *your* energy, instead of just worship. God would then be the generating energy of the life that is within you and within all things.

SOME OF the puberty initiations of the American Indian tribes were terribly painful ordeals. The young men were battered around and actually made to pass out in pain. And they'd pass out into bliss. This relationship of the two is a fundamentally logical theme. In our culture we're always thinking about ethics and morality and pain and the greatest good of the greatest number and all that. Nonsense! We forget that life doesn't give a damn about the greatest good of the greatest number! What it gives a damn about is that all should be in bliss!

WHEN LIFE becomes only problems, as in marriage, or with this silly chap, Hamlet—To be or not to be—then you're in a late stage of civilization and you're on the way down. Life has to be spontaneous. It has to come from what's called in India the *anandamayakosha*, the Sheath of Bliss. Life is an expression of bliss.

IN MY OWN teaching of 38 years at Sarah Lawrence, I saw this moment in many lives as I looked into those lovely young faces—new possibilities dawning for them—the decision. And then ten years later at alumni reunions, 20 years later, 30 years later, I would meet again these people...who had been my students. And it was not difficult to recognize who were the ones who had dared the adventure, and who were the ones who had not. If you do not dare the adventure you will enjoy a respectable, a very fine and noble life. If you do opt the adventure, you experience an interesting life. It will be full of danger, full of surprises,

full of shocks and disappointments,
but somehow as I saw in those eyes, a
freshness, a vitality has somehow gone
out of the others.

NOT ONLY IS the deity to become transparent to the transcendence, but so are *you*. I take the phrase from Karlfried Graf Dürckheim, a German philosopher and a great teacher. He was a healer, a psychiatrist, and he said, "Our minds carry us away from our nature—one of the functions of psychiatry and psychotherapy is to bring the Divine back into accord with our nature—and the source of the energies of our nature is transcendent of our knowledge; we don't know where it comes from." Your life is your experience of transcendent energies.

[ARTISTS] PROVIDE the contemporary metaphors that allow us to realize the transcendent, infinite, and abundant nature of being as it is.

I KNOW that the constant drumming of things around one can upset the pulse of one's heart. Environment can engulf us in pleasures and pains. But after all it's inside our own hearts that beauty reposes. Pleasures and pains affect the body; and if our dreamings have never released our souls, then pleasures and pains will upset our mental and emotional tranquility. Aggravations and disappointments—and even a certain blankness can help the soul to grow in understanding, once the soul has learned to feed upon whatever comes its way.

WHEN A MYTHIC dimension is opened to people, happiness, joy, and a sense of what might be called self-potentiality are opened to them as well. They have been given the saving image of human self-confidence and a new appreciation of the value of being a human being.

[**WRITING IS** a meditative act] for me. Meditation sounds complicated, but it's just waiting. I try not to publish anything that's from any other center. The wonderful thing is when I get on a certain beam that hits the level of mythic inspiration. From there on I know about three words ahead what I'm going to say. When the writing's going like that, I know I'm in the groove; it feels like riding a wonderful wave.

FIRST IS the mystical or metaphysical function of linking up regular waking consciousness with the vast mystery and wonder of the universe. This is the most essential service of a mythology, opening the mind and heart to the utter wonder of all being—arousing and maintaining in the individual a sense of awe and gratitude for the mystery of life, the mystery of existence, the mystery of the universe—which is the mystery of one's self.

SHEER LIFE cannot be said to have a purpose, because look at all the different purposes it has all over the place. But each incarnation, you might say, has a potentiality, and the mission of life is to live that potentiality. How do you do it? My answer is, "Follow your bliss." There's something inside

you that knows when you're in the center, that knows when you're on the beam or off the beam. And if you get off the beam to earn money, you've lost your life. And if you stay in the center and don't get any money, you still have your bliss.

[TO ACHIEVE BLISS] you've got to change [your thinking or your cognition]. This is the point that comes out all along the line in *Faust*. Goethe says Mephistopheles cannot control what Faust has done. All he can do is supply the means of Faust's achieving. But he cannot dictate what's to be achieved. When the Mental Sheath becomes the dictator, that's a diabolical life. That's life governed by concepts instead of the dynamic of life.

EVERY CIVILIZATION on the face of the earth has been shaped by a mythology. And the people who live in that world live in the atmosphere of myth. I noticed when I was in India the squalor, the horrible poverty—you can't believe it. It goes far beyond anything that our words refer to here. And yet a curious quality of peace and even bliss. Why? Because those people are accepting and living in a myth that supports them.

POETS ARE simply those who have made a profession and a lifestyle of being in touch with their bliss. Most people are concerned with other things. They get themselves involved in economic and political activities, or get drafted into a war that isn't the one they're interested in, and it may be difficult to hold to this umbilical under those circumstances. That is a technique each one has to work out for himself somehow. But most people living in that realm of what might be called occasional concerns have the capacity that is waiting to be awakened to move to this other field.

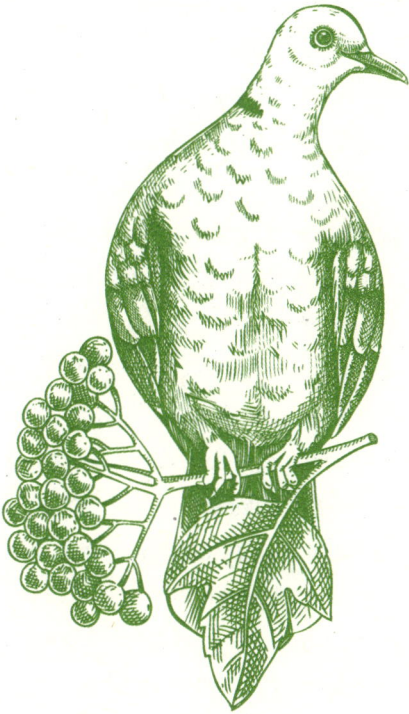

LISTEN TO YOUR DREAMS. Your conscious mind, your ego thinks it's running the show—you're doing things for this reason, and they mean that for you, and your dream tells you, "No, sir! This isn't what's running your life. You're making a mess out of it because I'm pushing you." Find out what that is. If you find your own chosen deity, what it is that is really cooking in your life, your life will be functioning in terms of that cooking whether you know what it is or not. But it helps to know who your god is and live with it. This is the great thing of finding your own dynamic.

REVOLUTION DOESN'T have to do with smashing something, it has to do with bringing something forth. If you spend all your time thinking about that which you are attacking, then you are negatively bound to it. You have to find the zeal in yourself and bring that out.

THE HERO may have to be brought back from his supernatural adventure by assistance from without. That is to say, the world may have to come and get him. For the bliss of the deep abode is not lightly abandoned in favor of the self-scattering of the wakened state.

YOU MAY HAVE a success in life, but then just think of it—what kind of life was it? What good was it—you've never done the thing you wanted to do in all your life. I always tell my students, go where your body and soul want to go. When you have the feeling, then stay with it, and don't let anyone throw you off.

YOUR TASK is to relate yourself to your world; not to some world that ought to be, not to some world that's somewhere else, but to *your* world. Find a position in it. And then, around the middle part of life you'll begin to find new dimensions of the spirit coming to you through the world in which you're living. And finally comes the drop-off, when you have to drop off, and you have then this rich second half of life thing that Jung talks about so well and that I know now because I'm well into it. It's something that comes along all by itself.

YOU LIVE your way honestly, with respect to yourself with integrity. And don't make more concessions to life than you have to; I mean to the life of the world as it's asking you to be.

MY WAY has been the way of bliss in reading. I will not finish a book that bores me, no matter how important it is. This has been my discipline. As a result, I have left unread a lot of things I ought to have read, and I have read many things I ought not to have read. (It is not respectable to admit it, but I have read everything Frobenius ever wrote.)

WE YEARN for something that never was on land or sea—namely, the fulfillment of that intelligible character that only the unique individual can bring forth. This is what Schopenhauer called "earned character." You bring forth what is potential within you and no one else.

YOU CAN NEVER become your own master until you find your own truth.... It is my belief that there is a very strong movement in the United States today to find—or at least for the *individual* to find in himself—that center, that centered and centering Eye. And perhaps if enough people discover it in themselves, it may be put to work in the government as well. But unless there are people who have come to the realization in themselves of the point at the center, beyond pairs of opposites, and the way of thinking in such terms, the principle of evenhandedness is not going to operate in public life. It has to be found first in private life. I would say that

whatever is about to occur in the way
of transformation of consciousness
will have had to have occurred, first, in
the hearts of individual human beings,
who will then have had—as a result of
their very presence—an influence in
the larger community.

THERE IS ONE phrase in *Finnegans Wake* that seems to me to epitomize the whole sense of Joyce. He says, "Oh lord, heap miseries upon us yet entwine our arts with laughters low." And this is the sense of the Buddhist Bodhisattva: joyful participation in the sorrows of the world.

WHAT THE RELATIONSHIP of the Father and the Son and the Holy Ghost to each other might be, in technical terms, is not half as important as you, the celebrant, feeling the virgin birth within you. The birth of the mystic, mythic being that is your own spiritual life.

THE REALIZATION of *tat tvam asi* ("you are that") [is what aligns Western philosophers with Eastern thought]. And you're there all the time! This is represented in the Bodhisattva ideal again epitomized in that beautiful phrase "joyful participation in the sorrows of the world." It's in the very field of sorrows that the disengagement from them, while participating in them voluntarily, is achieved. This is truly positive.

WE ARE having experiences all the time which may on occasion render some sense of this, a little intuition of where your bliss is. Grab it. No one can tell you what it is going to be. You have to learn to recognize your own depth.

FOR YEARS I've watched this whole business of young people deciding on their careers. There are only two attitudes: one is to follow your bliss; and the other is to read the projections as to where the money is going to be when you graduate. Well, it changes so fast. This year it's computer work; next year it's dentistry, and so on. And no matter what the young person decides, by the time he or she gets going, it will have changed. But if they have found where the center of their real bliss is, they can have that. You may not have money, but you'll have your bliss.

THE ADVENTURE is its own reward—but it's necessarily dangerous, having both negative and positive possibilities, all of them beyond control. We are following our own way, not our daddy's or our mother's way. So we are beyond protection in a field of higher powers than we know. One has to have some sense of what the conflict possibilities will be in this field, and here a few good archetypal stories like this may help us to know what to expect. If we have been impudent and altogether ineligible for the role into which we have cast ourselves, it is going to be a demon marriage and a real mess. However, even here there

may be heard a rescuing voice,
to convert the adventure into
a glory beyond anything ever
imagined.

I SAY, follow your bliss and don't be afraid, and doors will open where you didn't know they were going to be.

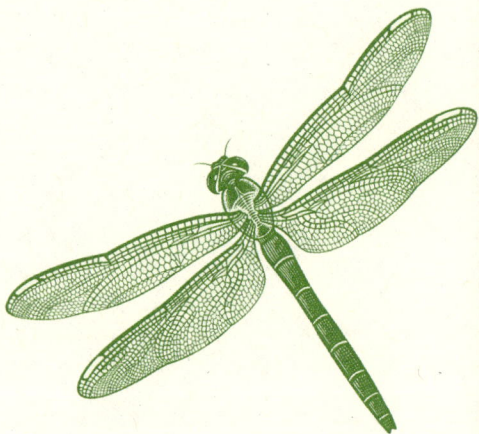

I DECIDED long ago I wouldn't do a goddamn thing I didn't want to do. My father's hosiery business was in very bad condition in the Crash. I didn't know where I was. The world had blown open. I'm no longer in the PhD bottle. I don't want to go on with my little Arthurian pieces. I had *much* more exciting things to do—and I didn't know what they were. I wanted to write, I wanted to be an anthropologist—I didn't know *what*! A new wonder was around. So I said, "To hell with it, Columbia!" I didn't have a job for five years!

VISHNU AT THE END of the world
appears as a monster. There he is,
destroying the universe, first with fire
and then with a torrential flood that
drowns out the fire and everything
else. Nothing is left but ash. The whole
universe with all its life and lives has
been utterly wiped out. That's God in
the role of destroyer. Such experiences
go past ethical or aesthetic judgments.
Ethics is wiped out. Whereas in our
religions, with their accent on the
human, there is also an accent on the
ethical—God is qualified as good. No,
no! God is horrific. Any god who can
invent hell is no candidate for the
Salvation Army. The end of the world,
think of it! But there is a Muslim saying

about the Angel of Death: "When the Angel of Death approaches, he is terrible. When he reaches you, it is bliss."

THERE'S NOTHING you can do that's more important than being fulfilled. You become a sign, you become a signal, transparent to transcendence; in this way, you will find, live, and become a realization of your own personal myth.

WE'RE SO AFRAID of this or that threat which may or may not come. If it doesn't come, so what? If it does, so what? When people *know* that they're going to die in a few months or even weeks, they become so alert and aware of the present—and then they begin to more fully experience it. To live with the anxiety of a future calamity, when all the joys of the present moment are asking to be recognized, seems to me a good way to miss the show.

SURVIVAL, SECURITY, personal relationships, prestige, self-development— in my experience, those are exactly the values that a mythically inspired person *doesn't* live for.

THE LADY of the House of Sleep is a familiar figure in fairy tale and myth.... She is the paragon of all paragons of beauty, the reply to all desire, the bliss-bestowing goal of every hero's earthly and unearthly quest. She is mother, sister, mistress, bride. Whatever in the world has lured, whatever has seemed to promise joy, has been premonitory of her existence—in the deep of sleep, if not in the cities and forests of the world. For she is the incarnation of the promise of perfection; the soul's assurance that, at the conclusion of its exile in a world of organized inadequacies, the bliss that once was known will be known again; the comforting, the nourishing, the "good" mother—young and beautiful—who was known to us, and even tasted, in the remotest past. Time sealed her away, yet she is dwelling still, like one who sleeps in timelessness, at the bottom of the timeless sea.

TO RISE then along the mounting scale from one glory to the next, one has only to face and dare to enter the lion's mouth: the flaming sun door of the present, absorbed totally in the living here-and-now, without hope, without fear. Whereupon the rapture of the Muses—the arts—will begin to be experienced in the body of this world itself, transporting our spirit from glory to glory, to that summit of joy in consciousness where the world eye—beyond hope, beyond fear—surveys the universe in its coming, going, and being.

I THOUGHT, "I don't know whether my consciousness is proper consciousness or not; I don't know whether what I know of my being is my proper being or not; but I do know where my rapture is. So let me hang on to rapture, and that will bring me both my consciousness and my being." I think it worked.

THERE'S A European word, *werden*
in German, "to become." You become
what you are potentially to be. And
that *werden*, "to become," is at the root
of the word *weird*. This is translated
as "fate," but it's very different from
kismet. It appears in *Beowulf*, the
earliest English epic, when Beowulf, as
an old warrior, is about to go against
the dragon, and he knows he isn't up
to it. But it's what his destiny is to do;
he's the chieftain, after all, and nobody
else can go in on that dragon. There's
a line that, to me, is one of the most
telling lines in Anglo-Saxon literature:
"Wyrd was very near." He's sitting,

thinking, pulling himself together to go into this battle. "Wyrd"—the terminal moment of his *werden*, his becoming.

WHEN I WAS a student in Paris I met and came to know as a teacher and friend the great sculptor Antoine Bourdelle; I remember him saying to his students: *"L'art fait ressortir les grandes lignes de la nature"* ("Art brings out the grand lines of nature"). And these grand lines are irreducibly informed by death, suffering, and sorrow. The artist's eye views, affirms, and participates in all this—beyond fear and desire. And mythology moves us from that aesthetic level to the realization of transcendence.

IF YOU TAKE a journey that's not proper to your needs, it's going to be a wreck all the way. The main clue to living your life is, follow your bliss. When you're really in bliss, that's your path. And don't worry that things won't come your way. They will. Doors will open where they weren't before. This is the way of life that the hero must gain.

THE COMMON MAN, in pain, believes that by altering his circumstances he might achieve a state free of pain: his world, in Gottfried's phrase, being of those who want only "to bathe in bliss."

WHEN YOU FOLLOW the path of your desire and enthusiasm and emotion, keep your mind in control, and don't let it pull you compulsively into disaster.

EXPERIENCE, not concept, is the way to the divine. This business of taking your way, your folk idea of the deity, as representing *the* deity, is to miss the point. As the old Gnostics used to say, "The problem with Yahweh is he thinks he's God." He is a reference to a mystery. The mystic philosopher Meister Eckhart, in the thirteenth and fourteenth centuries, says, "The ultimate leave-taking is leaving God for God"; that is to say, leaving your folk idea, the ethnic idea—the historical notion, with words and pictures to explain—for that which is inexplicable, that which transcends (what the Hindus call "that which no tongue has soiled, no word has reached"), and yet can be experienced as moving within oneself, and also as moving within the field of time round about.

WHEN A POET carries the mind into a context of meanings and then pitches it past those, one knows that marvelous rapture that comes from going past all categories of definition.

VIRTUE IS but the pedagogical prelude to the culminating insight, which goes beyond all pairs of opposites. Virtue quells the self-centered ego and makes the transpersonal centeredness possible; but when that has been achieved, what then of the pain or pleasure, vice or virtue, either of our own ego or of any other? Through all, the transcendent force is then perceived which lives in all, in all is wonderful, and is worthy, in all, of our profound obeisance.

THE PHILOSOPHICAL formula illustrated by the cosmogonic cycle is that of the circulation of consciousness through the three planes of being. The first plane is that of waking experience: cognitive of the hard, gross facts of an outer universe, illuminated by the light of the sun, and common to all. The second plane is that of dream experience: cognitive of the fluid, subtle forms of a private interior world, self-luminous and of one substance with the dreamer. The third plane is that of deep sleep: dreamless, profoundly blissful. In the first are encountered the instructive experiences of life; in the second these are digested, assimilated to the inner forces of the dreamer; while in the third all is enjoyed and known unconsciously, in the "space within the heart," the room of the inner controller, the source and end of all.

AND THE FALL in the Garden occurred when Adam and Eve knew the difference between good and evil. That's the way to get out of the land of bliss. The way back is to go to that tree again that was there before the knowledge of good and evil, the tree in the middle of the Garden, which is between the pairs of opposites.

THAT'S WHAT PEOPLE are doing all over the place—dying for metaphors. But when you really realize the sound, "AUM," the sound of the mystery of the word everywhere, then you don't have to go out and die for anything because it's right there all around. Just sit still and see it and experience it and know it. That's a peak experience.... That's right, and that's why it is a peak experience to break past all that, every now and then, and to realize, "Oh... ah..."

IN BUDDHIST SYSTEMS, more especially those of Tibet, the meditation Buddhas appear in two aspects, one peaceful and the other wrathful. If you are clinging fiercely to your ego and its little temporal world of sorrows and joys, hanging on for dear life, it will be the wrathful aspect of the deity that appears. It will seem terrifying. But the moment your ego yields and gives up, that same meditation Buddha is experienced as a bestower of bliss.

FINALLY, the world destruction, which the physicists tell us must come with the exhaustion of our sun and ultimate running down of the whole cosmos, stands presaged in the scar left by the fire of Tangaroa: the world-destructive effects of the creator-destroyer will increase gradually until, at last, in the second course of the cosmogonic cycle, all will devolve into the sea of bliss.

SOURCE TEXTS

"Civilization and Its Discontents: The
    Vitality of Myth" (lecture)
"Classical Mysteries of the Great Goddess"
    (seminar)
Correspondence: 1927–1987
The Hero with a Thousand Faces
*The Hero's Journey: Joseph Campbell on
    His Life and Work*
"Jungian Psychology and Archetypes of
    Mythology" (lecture)
*The Masks of God, Volume 4: Creative
    Mythology*
*Myth and Meaning: Conversations on
    Mythology and Life*
*Pathways to Bliss: Mythology and Personal
    Transformation*
The Power of Myth
*Thou Art That: Transforming Religious
    Metaphor*

ABOUT JOSEPH CAMPBELL

Joseph Campbell (1904–1987) was a renowned American author and scholar of comparative mythology. His groundbreaking work *The Hero with a Thousand Faces* (1949) introduced the concept of the "hero's journey," a universal pattern found in myths across cultures. Campbell's theories were influenced by his studies in Europe, the work of Picasso and Joyce, Freud's and Jung's theories about the human psyche, his lifelong interest in Native American cultures, and his translation with Swami Nikhilananda of the Upanishads and *The Gospel of Sri Ramakrishna*. In 1988, the PBS series *The Power of Myth* brought his ideas to a global audience, solidifying his legacy in the study of mythology.